# Our Seasons

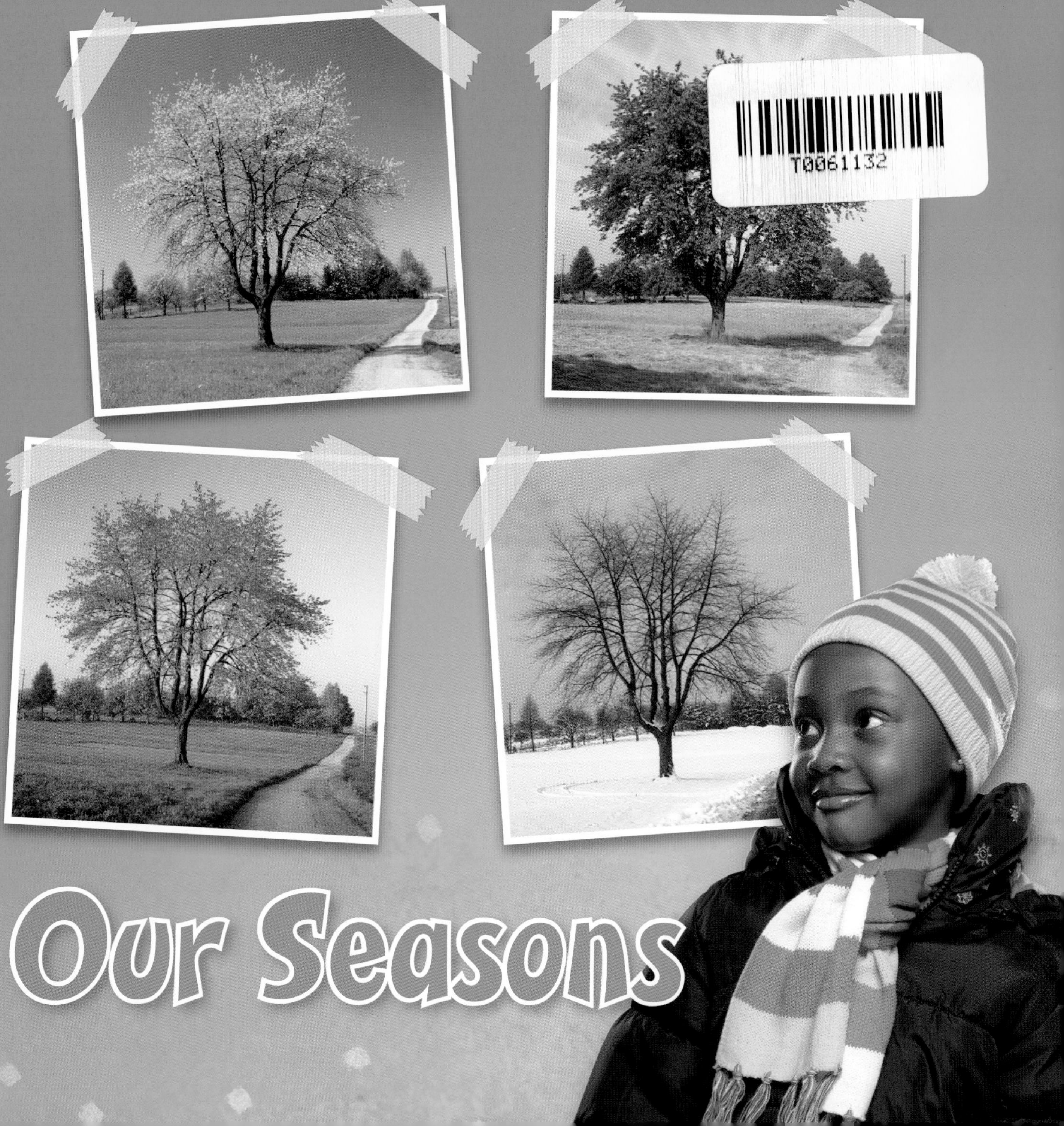

T0061132

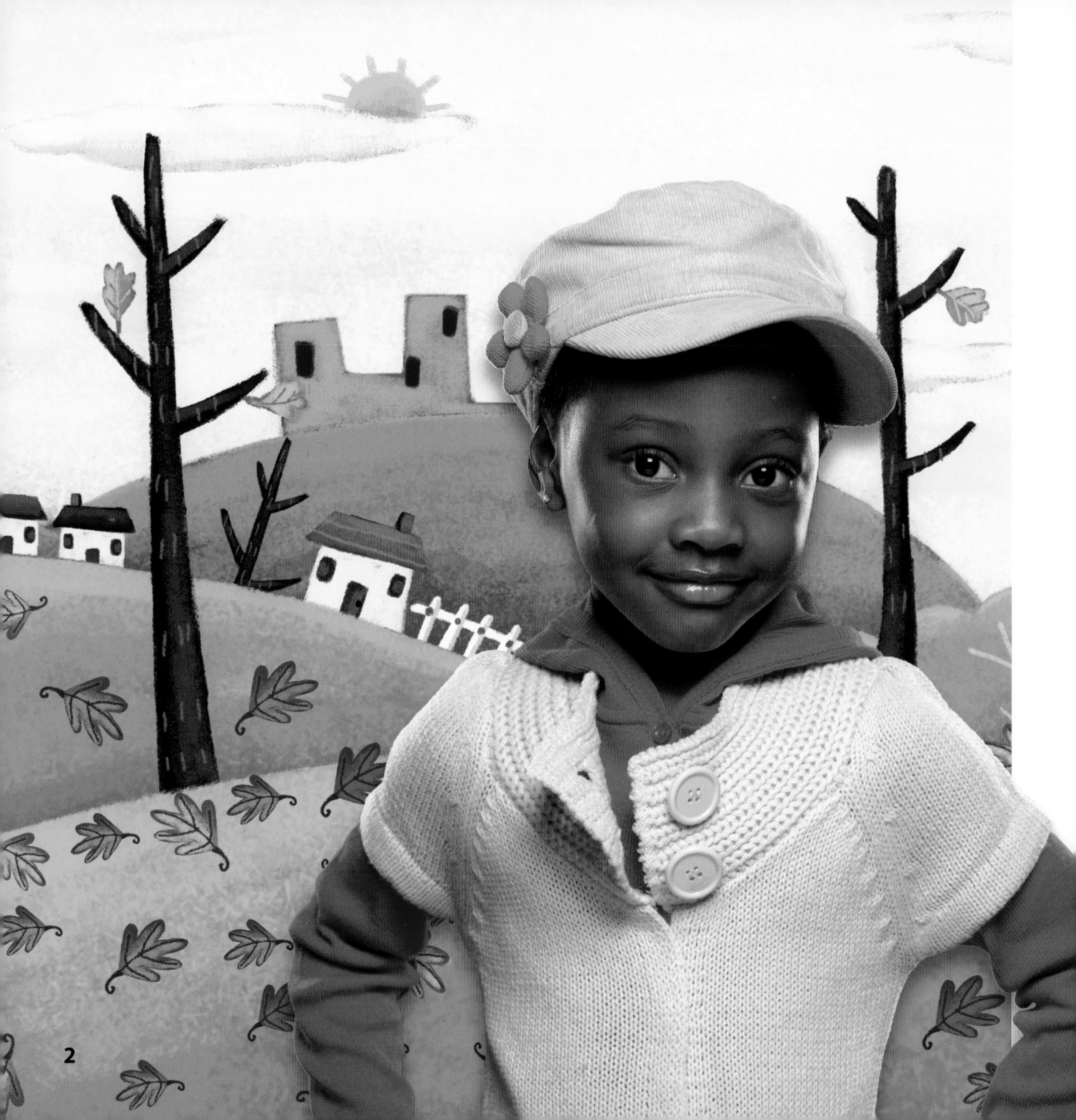

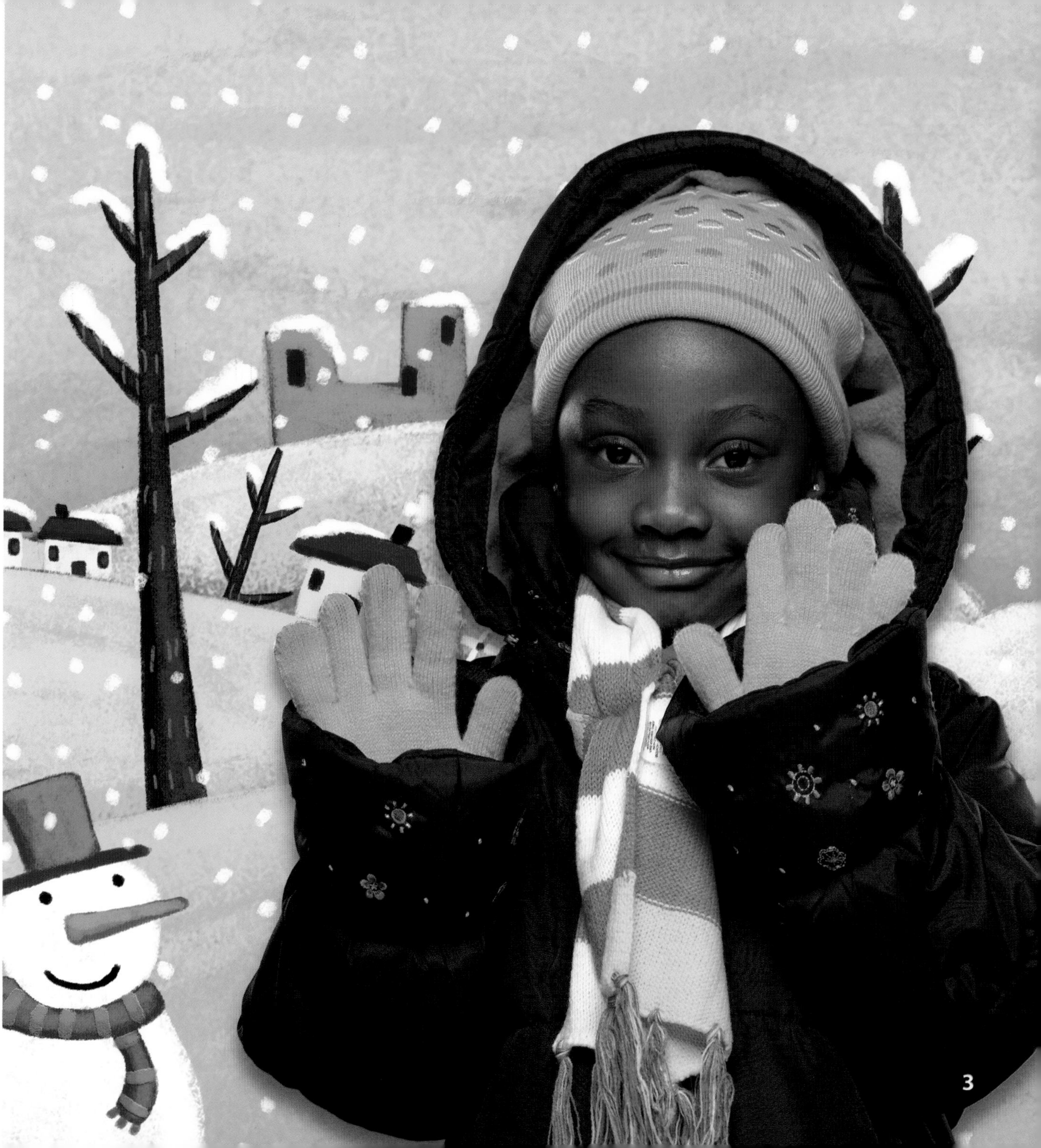

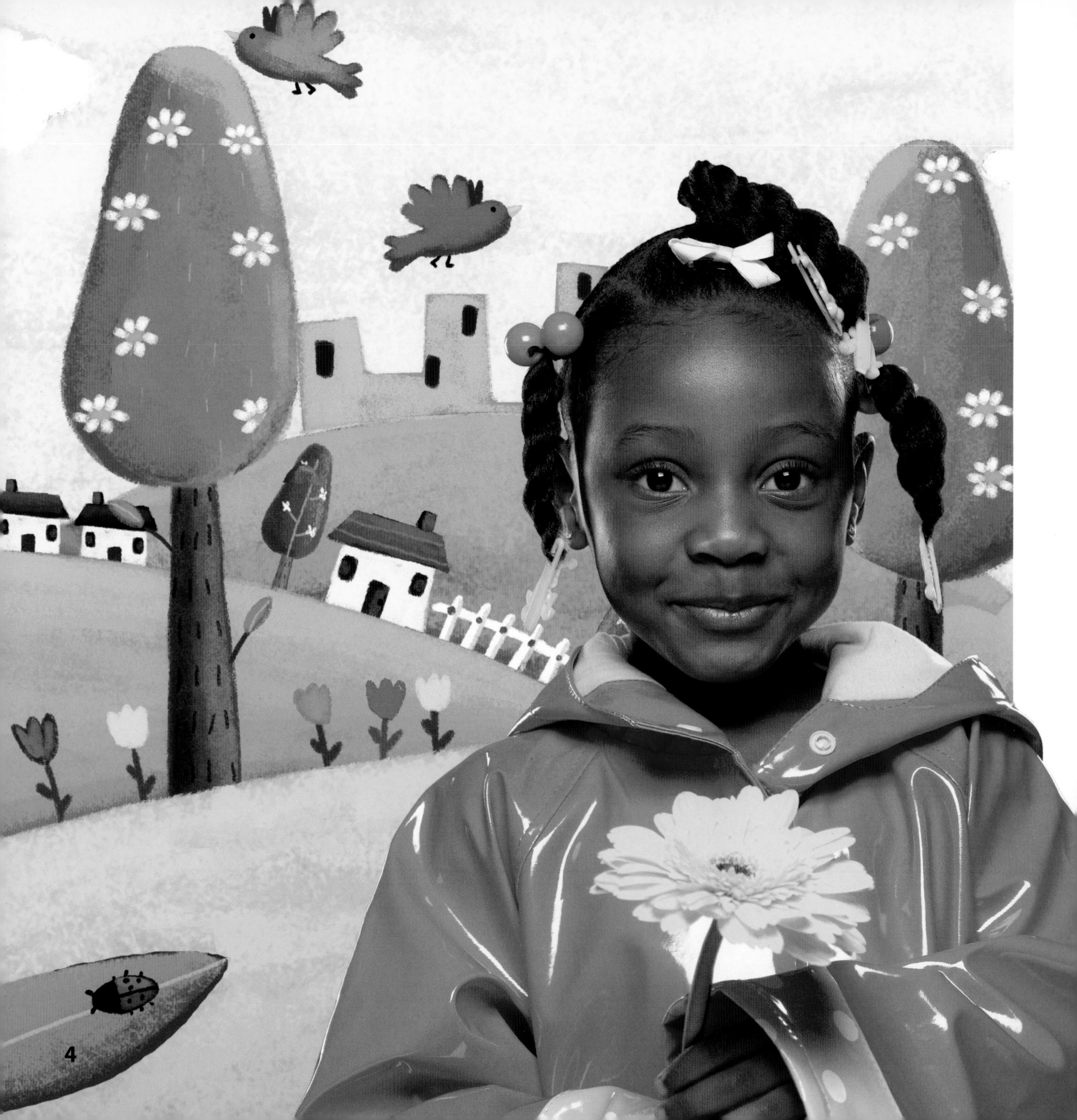

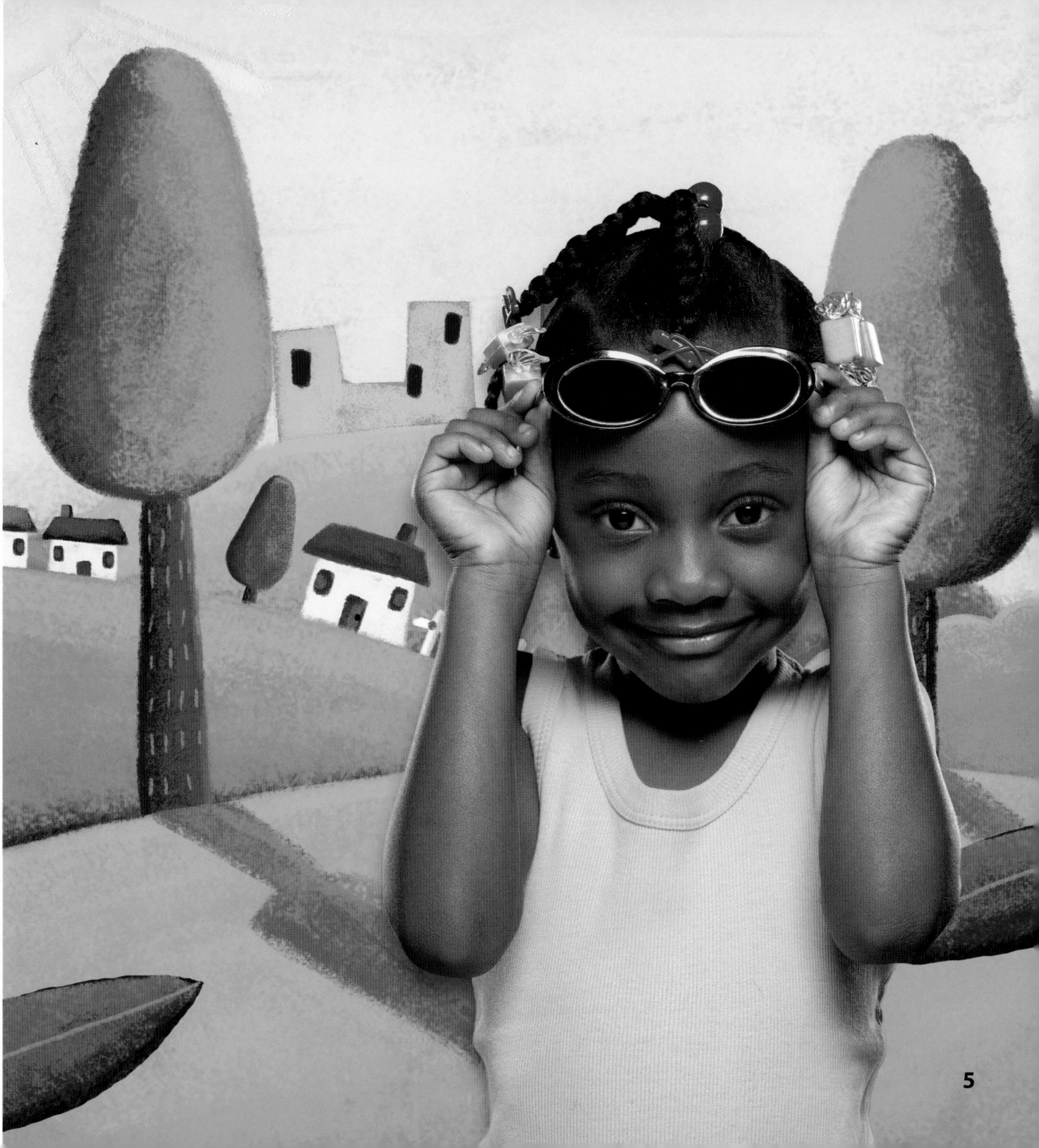

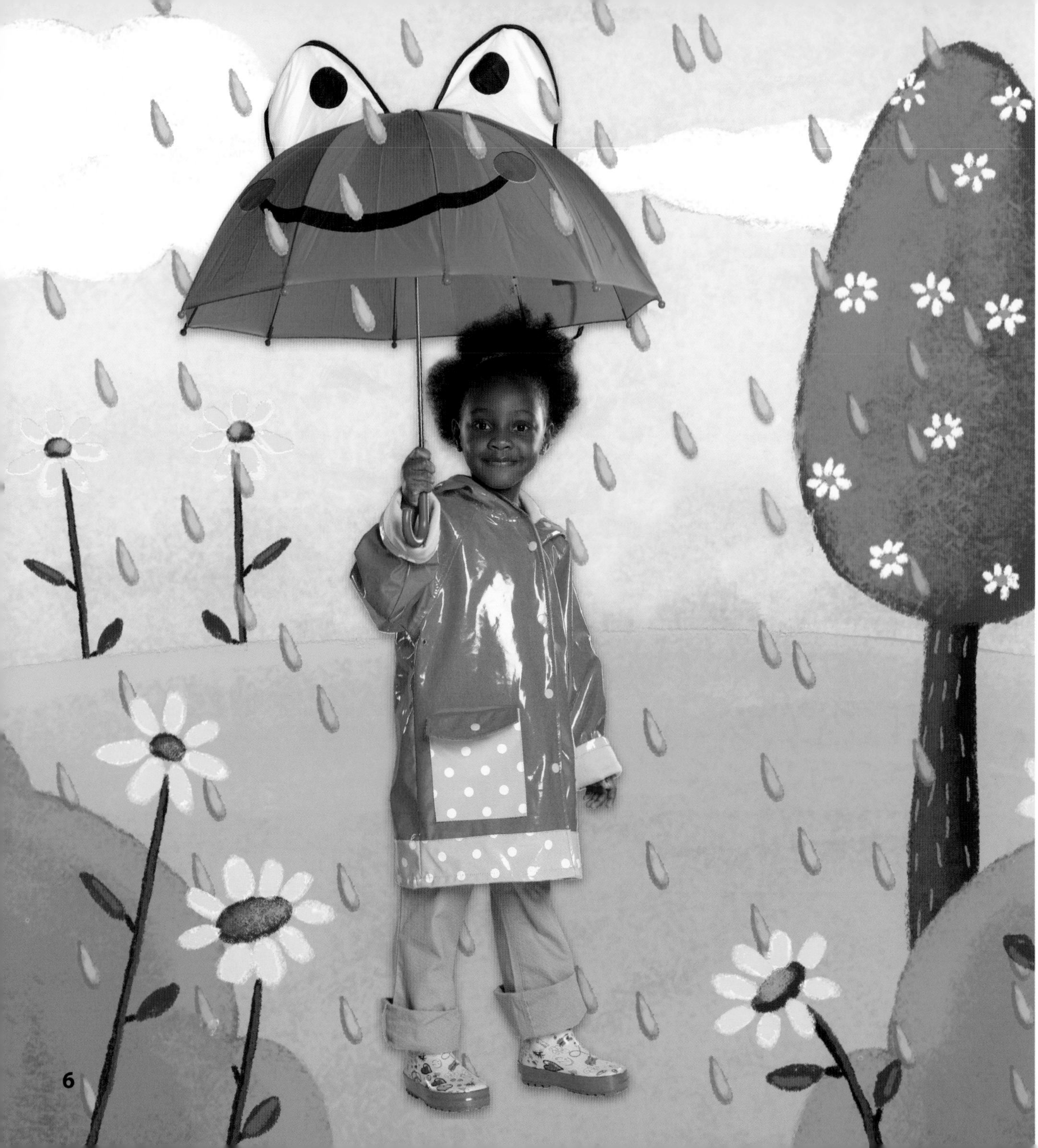

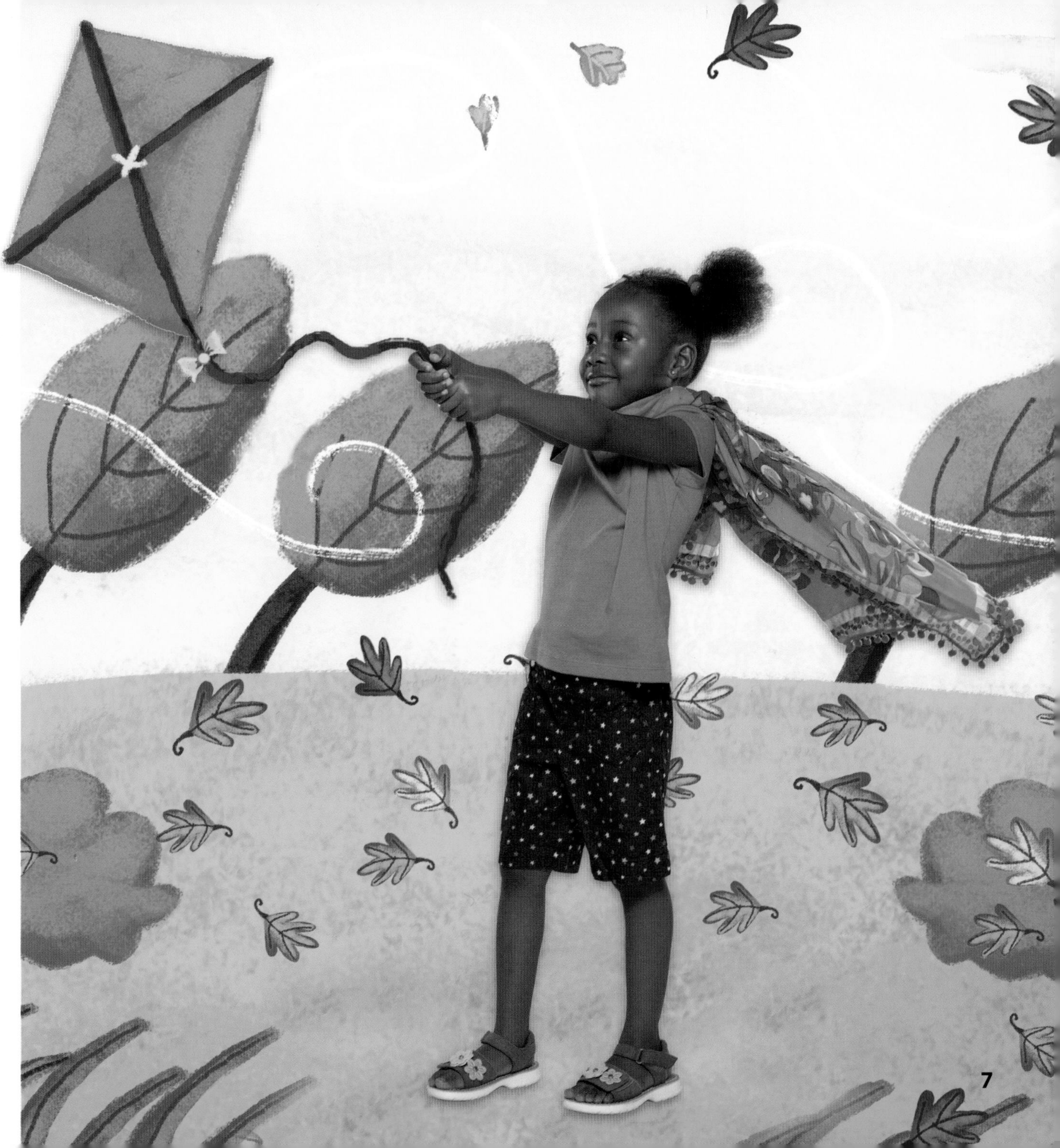

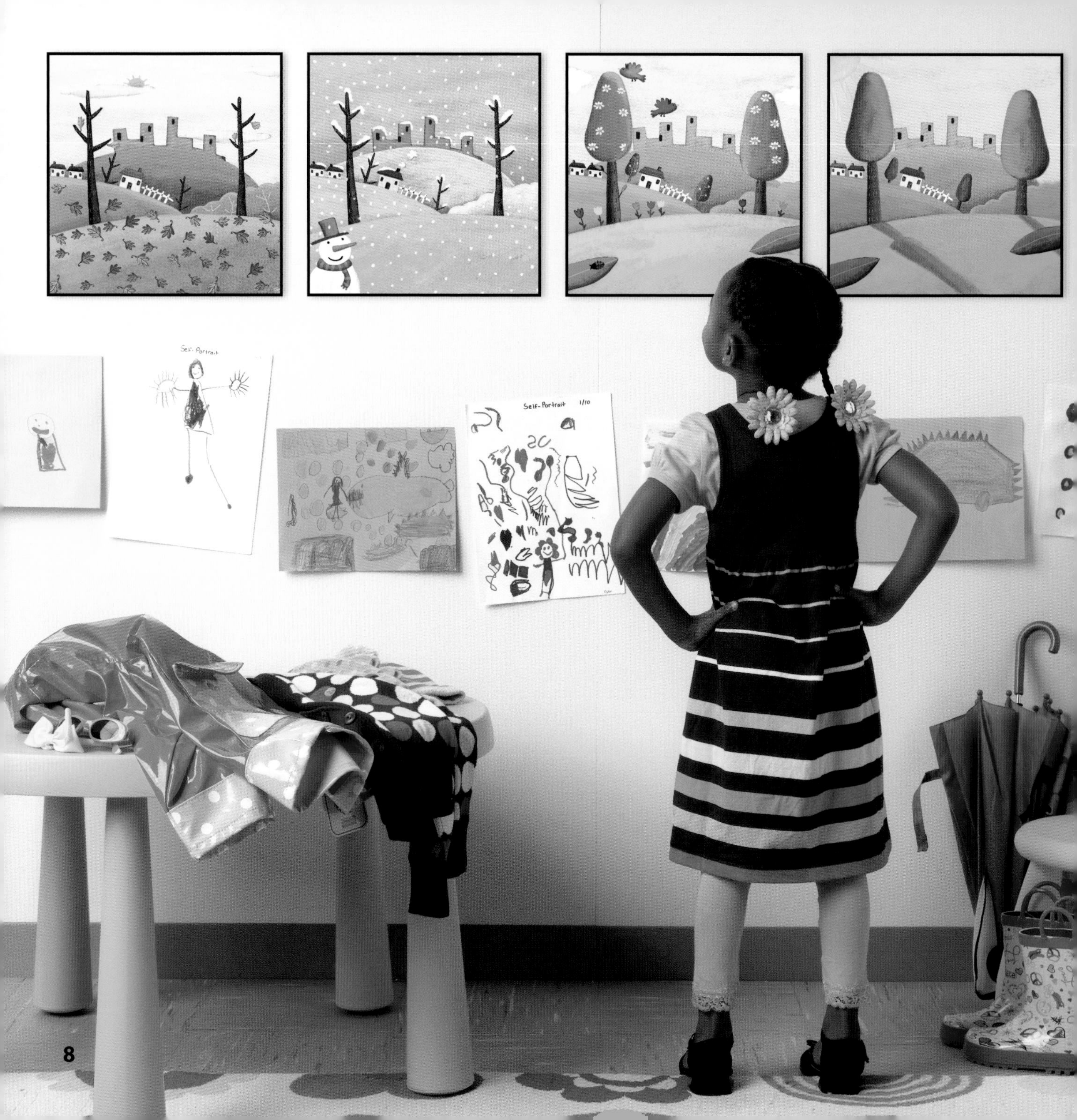
Self-Portrait
Self-Portrait 1/10